20-

D1294608

THE BLACK DEATH

BY MARY GRIFFIN

Gareth Stevens
PUBLISHING

CRASHCOURSE

Please visit our website, www.garethstevens.com. For a free color catalog of all our high-quality books, call toll free 1-800-542-2595 or fax 1-877-542-2596.

Library of Congress Cataloging-in-Publication Data

Names: Griffin, Mary, 1978- author.
Title: The Black Death / Mary Griffin.
Description: New York : Gareth Stevens Publishing, [2020] | Series: A look at world history | Includes bibliographical references and index.
Identifiers: LCCN 2018039206| ISBN 9781538241264 (pbk.) | ISBN 9781538241288 (library bound) | ISBN 9781538241271 (6 pack)
Subjects: LCSH: Black Death--Europe--History--Juvenile literature. | Plague--History--Juvenile literature. | Epidemics--Europe--History--14th century--Juvenile literature. | Diseases and history--Juvenile literature. | Europe--History--14th century--Juvenile literature.
Classification: LCC RA644.P7 G75 2019 | DDC 614.5/732/094--dc23
LC record available at https://lccn.loc.gov/2018039206

First Edition

Published in 2020 by
Gareth Stevens Publishing
111 East 14th Street, Suite 349
New York, NY 10003

OCT 0 2 2019

Copyright © 2020 Gareth Stevens Publishing

Designer: Katelyn E. Reynolds
Editor: Therese Shea

Photo credits: Cover, p. 1 Bettmann/Getty Images; cover, pp. 1–32 (background) javarman/Shutterstock.com; cover, pp. 1–32 (border) Anastasiia Smiian/Shutterstock.com; pp. 5, 29 DEA /A. DAGLI ORTI/De Agostini Picture Library/Getty Images; p. 7 DEA /R. MERLO/De Agostini/Getty Images; p. 9 (inset) Smith Collection/Gado/Getty Images; p. 9 (main) BSIP/UIG via Getty Images; p. 11 PD-USGov-HHS-CDC/ Optigan13/Wikipedia.org; p. 13 Science Photo Library/Getty Images; p. 15 Andrei Minsk/Shutterstock.com; p. 17 NYPL/Science Source/Getty Images; p. 19 Archiv Gerstenberg/ullstein bild via Getty Images; p. 21 MOLA/Getty Images; p. 23 Ann Ronan Pictures/Print Collector/Getty Images; p. 25 Leemage/Corbis via Getty Images; p. 27 anonymous (Queen Mary Master)/Il Dottore/Wikipedia.org; p. 30 Master of Puppets and Alexrk2/Wikipedia.org.

Printed in the United States of America

CPSIA compliance information: Batch #CS19GS: For further information contact Gareth Stevens, New York, New York at 1-800-542-2595.

CONTENTS

Words in the glossary appear in **bold** type the first time they are used in the text.

DEADLY DISEASE

The Black Death sounds like the name of a creepy movie, but it was a real-life event. The Black Death was the terrible spread of **plague** throughout Europe and Asia during the 1300s. Before it was over, millions of people had died.

MAKE THE GRADE

An epidemic is a sudden, unexpected increase in
the number of people with a disease, or illness.
A pandemic is an epidemic across several
countries. The Black Death was a pandemic.

5

BROUGHT BY BOAT

Twelve ships arrived in Messina, Sicily, off the coast of Italy, in October 1347. The people who met the ships were frightened by what they saw. The sailors were covered in black boils, or **swollen** areas under the skin. Most were dead.

MESSINA urbs est Siciliæ maxima, situ, opulentia, & tuta nauium statione, in qua mirabilis naturæ vis apparet, celeberrima: ab Italia, seua Charybdi discreta, ab occasum mare firma, publicis priuatisq; ædificijsq; cultis, fonte perenni, antiquissimis statuae, signis, & scriarum ciuium theatris, nobilissima.

MAKE THE GRADE

The disease the sailors brought to Europe had been reported in China, India, Persia (today's Iran), Syria, and Egypt in the early 1340s.

7

WHAT WAS IT?

What was this terrible sickness? At the time, no one knew. Most scientists today think it was plague caused by a bacterium called *Yersinia pestis*. Many think it was spread by rats that had been bitten by **infected** fleas.

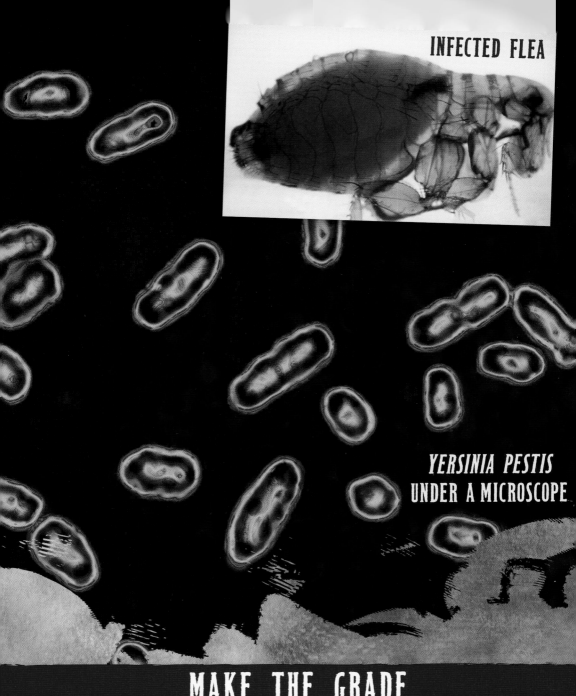

INFECTED FLEA

YERSINIA PESTIS
UNDER A MICROSCOPE

MAKE THE GRADE

Some scientists think the Black Death
was spread by fleas and lice
that lived on people!

There are three kinds of plague. Bubonic plague is named for the buboes, or swellings in the **glands**, that it causes. Pneumonic (noo-MAHN-ihk) plague affects the lungs. Septicemic (sehp-teh-SEE-mihk) plague attacks the bloodstream. Septicemic plague is the deadliest form.

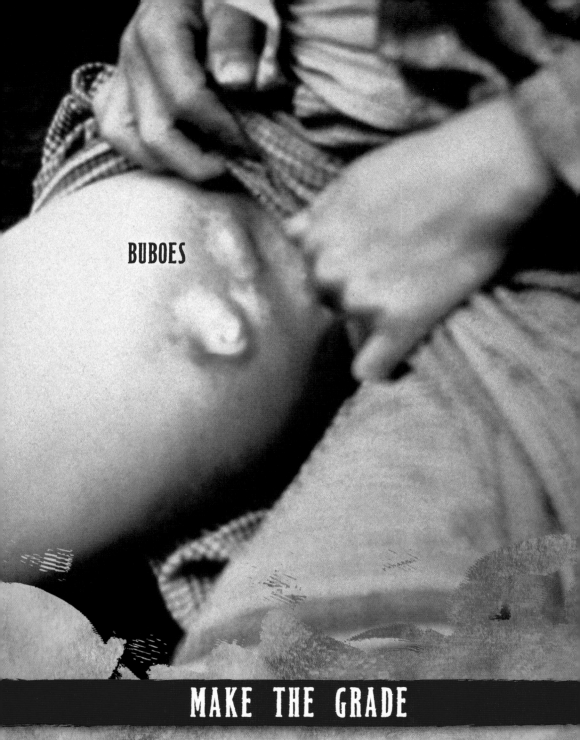

BUBOES

MAKE THE GRADE

Some think the Black Death involved
more than one kind of plague.

After someone was infected by the Black Death, certain parts of their body swelled. Blood and **pus** leaked from these growths. An infected person might feel hot or cold. They might throw up and have terrible aches and pains. Finally, they might die.

MAKE THE GRADE

Septicemic plague could kill someone
in less than 24 hours!

13

DEATH SPREADS

Infected fleas and rats were
on many ships, so the Black
Death easily spread wherever
these ships went. But no one
at the time knew how the
plague was spreading. After
it struck Sicily, it traveled
to ports in France, Italy,
and North Africa. It was in
England by 1348.

14

TRADE ROUTES DURING
THE BLACK DEATH

EUROPE

PERSIA

CHINA

ARABIA

INDIA

AFRICA

INDIAN OCEAN

— LAND ROUTES
— SEA ROUTES

MAKE THE GRADE

It's thought the Black Death started
somewhere in China or Central Asia.
It probably spread from there
through trade routes.

15

TERRIBLE TREATMENT

During the 1300s, doctors knew little about sicknesses. They thought plague traveled through the air. To treat it, they bled **patients** and cut buboes. These treatments sometimes killed patients before plague did. **Herbs** and special baths were harmless but not helpful.

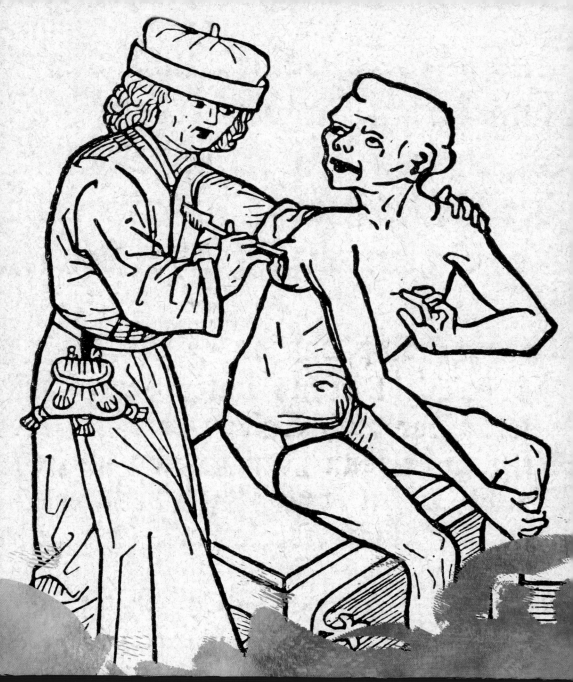

MAKE THE GRADE

One doctor said people
could get plague just by
looking at someone who had it!

17

Many doctors wouldn't even try to treat people with plague. Some frightened families left their loved ones to die alone. The Black Death killed men and women, young and old, and rich and poor. Even kings and queens died.

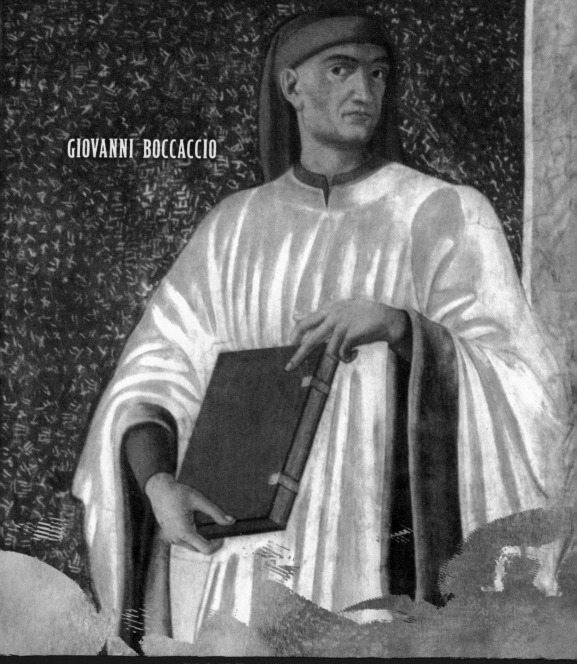

GIOVANNI BOCCACCIO

MAKE THE GRADE

Some of the ideas we have about
the Black Death come from an
Italian writer named Giovanni Boccaccio,
who lived around that time.

19

So many people died of
plague each day during the
Black Death that the dead
were gathered up each night.
They were buried together
in large graves called plague
pits. Some of these pits are
still being unearthed today!

MAKE THE GRADE

Scientists can study human remains
to find out what killed them.
Yersinia pestis has been
found in teeth!

21

WHO'S TO BLAME?

Some people thought the Black Death was a **punishment** from God for their sins. They marched through towns several times a day, praying and hitting themselves. This was their way of asking God for forgiveness. These people were called flagellants (FLA-jeh-lentz).

MAKE THE GRADE

Since **religion** didn't stop plague
from spreading, some turned
against religion altogether.

23

Many Christians blamed Jewish people for causing the Black Death. They thought Jews poisoned the wells where they got their water. Thousands of Jews were killed. Thousands more ran away from their homes to escape **persecution**.

MAKE THE GRADE

Jews were less affected by plague
because they lived in communities
apart from infected people.

25

DEATH BRINGS CHANGE

The Black Death probably killed about one-third of all people in Europe. It changed the world. Europeans had lived under the **feudal system**. Most were poor and worked the land of the rich. With fewer people left to do the work, laborers **demanded** better treatment.

26

MAKE THE GRADE

Historians believe about 25 million people
in Europe died during the Black Death.
Perhaps three times as many died in Asia.

27

MORE PLAGUES

The Black Death finally disappeared in the 1350s. However, it came back every few years. Since people still lived in unclean conditions, plague bacteria continued to spread. In fact, plague still occurs today. Luckily, doctors now know how to fight it.

MAKE THE GRADE

The Black Death was a subject of
many works of art. These help us learn
what happened during this time in history.

29

THE SPREAD OF THE
BLACK DEATH

1351

1350

MINOR
OUTBREAK

1349

1348

1347

GLOSSARY

demand: to ask in a forceful way

feudal system: a social system that existed in Europe during the Middle Ages in which people worked and fought for nobles who gave them protection and the use of land in return

gland: a body part that produces something needed for a bodily function

herb: a low-growing plant used to add flavor to food

infected: having something harmful inside the body

patient: a person who receives medical care or treatment

persecution: making a group of people suffer cruel or unfair treatment

plague: a disease that causes death and that spreads quickly to a large number of people

punishment: a way of making someone suffer for wrongdoing

pus: a thick, yellowish matter produced when a part of the body becomes infected

religion: a belief in and way of honoring a god or gods

swollen: larger than normal, sometimes because of an illness

FOR MORE INFORMATION

BOOKS

Farndon, John. *Plague!* Minneapolis, MN: Hungry Tomato, 2017.

Jeffrey, Gary. *The Black Death*. New York, NY: Crabtree Publishing Company, 2014.

WEBSITE

Black Death
www.dkfindout.com/us/history/black-death/
Read more about life during this deadly time.

INDEX